CANDLE HISTORY OF THE BIBLE

Published by
Lion Hudson Limited
Wilkinson House, Jordan Hill Business Park,
Banbury Road, Oxford OX2 8DR, England
www.lionhudson.com

ISBN 978 1 78128 316 5

First edition 2019

A catalogue record for this book is available
from the British Library

Printed and bound in China, May 2019, LH54

Text acknowledgements
Unless otherwise indicated, all Scripture quotations are taken from the Holy Bible, New International Version Anglicised. Copyright © 1979, 1984, 2011 Biblica, formerly International Bible Society. Used by permission of Hodder & Stoughton Ltd, an Hachette UK company. All rights reserved. "NIV" is a registered trademark of Biblica. UK trademark number 1448790. Scriptures quotations marked GNB are from the Good News Bible © 1994 published by the Bible Societies/HarperCollins Publishers Ltd UK, Good News Bible© American Bible Society 1966, 1971, 1976, 1992. Used with permission. Foreign language translations of Psalm 23 on pp.60-61 © United Bible Societies.

Picture acknowledgements
Every effort has been made to contact the illustrators of this work, although this has not been possible in all cases. If notified, the publisher will rectify any errors or omissions at the earliest opportunity.

Illustrations
Alan Parry pp.5, 60
Ann Baum p.19
Gary Rees p.57 (Liddell)
Illustrated London News p.37 (Tischendorf)
Martin Salisbury p.56 (Francis)
Pamela Goodchild pp.52, 53
Peter Dennis pp.3/38 (scribes), 3/50 (Lefèvre d'Étaples)/front cover/back cover, 22, 23 (except Paul), 24 (except hinged boards), 25, 26, 27, 29 (cuneiform), 32 (fragment), 33 (Hebrew scrolls), 34 (jars), 36, 39/front cover, 41/front cover (main image), 42 (ship), 45, 46 (printers), 49 (except Bible), 51 (translators), 54 (office), 56 (Livingstone)
Richard Scott pp.3/8 (Elijah), 10 (David), 11, 12, 13, 14 (messenger), 15, 16 (Temple), 17, 18, 21, 23 (Paul), 24 (hinged boards), 29 (scribe), 33 (copper scrolls), 42 (monk), 63
Shirley Bellwood p.20
Tony Morris pp.31, 32 (manuscript), 44, 47 (Erasmus), 48 (burning), 54 (Mary Jones)

Photographs
Dreamstime pp. 3/4-5 (header)/back cover Nexus7; 3/14 (temple)/back cover Suateracar; 3/30 (yad) Blueenayim; 3/35 (Hebrew)/front cover/back cover Byjeng; 3/40 (Amharic)/back cover Dmitry Chulov; 3/58 (family)/front cover Kostiantyn Gerashchenko; 6 Igor Zakharevich; 10 (archers) Radiokafka; 28 Perseomedusa; 32 (alphabet) Georgios Kollidas; 40 (Syriac) Capa34; 43 Pancaketom; 46 (Bible) Spaceheater; 47 (Gutenberg) Claudiodivizia; 48 Weber11; 49 (Bible) Awcnz62; 50 (statue) Amalteyka; 55 Oleksandr Solonenko; 59 Karl Daniels; 62 Kevin Carden
Tim Dowley Associates: pp.34 (caves)/back cover, 35 (remains)/front cover, 37 (monastery), 51

CANDLE HISTORY OF THE BIBLE

Dr Tim Dowley

CANDLE BOOKS

CONTENTS

The Jews are often known as "People of the Book". This Jewish teacher or "rabbi" is instructing young boys in the Jewish Scriptures.

What is the Bible?

Most Christians' beliefs are based on the Bible. But what exactly is the Bible? And how did it come into being?

The Bible is made up of a "library" of 66 books: 39 in the Old Testament and 27 in the New Testament.

Old Testament

The writings of the Old Testament first appeared as separate scrolls, mainly written in Hebrew. The 39 books of the Old Testament are by a number of different authors. They include different styles of writing and varied contents. They can be divided into four major groups:

1. Law

These books are sometimes called the "five scrolls" ("Pentateuch") or the Books of Moses. Followers of the Jewish religion (Judaism) call this section "The Books of the Law" or "Torah". The five books tell the story of God's people from Abraham to Moses. They also include the Creation story, Noah's Flood, the "Exodus", and the giving of the Ten Commandments.

2. History

These books trace the story of God's people from their entry into the Promised Land, led by Joshua, the setting up of the Kingdom of Israel and the division into two kingdoms, to their defeat by Babylon and Persia, and foreign exile.

3. Poetry and Wisdom

Songs of worship, love poetry, wise sayings, proverbs, riddles, parables, and warnings are gathered together in these books.

4. Prophecy

God's prophets, such as Isaiah, Daniel, and Jeremiah, explained what had happened in the past, spoke out against evil in the present, and told something about what God would do in the future.

New Testament

The 27 books of the New Testament were originally written in Greek. They too can be divided into different types of writing:

1. History

The four Gospels, however, are not simply historical records. They were also written to persuade readers to believe in Jesus, and form portraits of Jesus the Messiah. They are based on eye-witness accounts of Jesus' life, death, and resurrection. The Book of Acts tells how the earliest churches started and grew rapidly.

2. Letters

These include the apostle Paul's 13 letters to churches in various cities and to individual Christians, and letters written by other apostles.

3. Revelation

This book opens with letters to seven churches in Asia Minor (modern Turkey). It continues with visions about the last days that foretell the final victory of Christ and his church.

The Apocrypha

The Apocrypha is a collection of books and additions to the Old Testament books written between 300 BC and AD 100. These books were not accepted by the Jews as part of their Scriptures. Most Protestant churches don't regard them as part of Scripture. However, they are interesting, and range from books of history to holy fiction.

What's in the Books of the Old Testament?

Noah releases a dove from the ark.

Moses and his brother Aaron deliver God's message to Pharaoh: "Let my people go!"

GENESIS

This book of beginnings includes Creation, Adam and Eve disobeying God, and Noah and the great flood. It is the early story of God's people and his plans to save humankind.

EXODUS

This is the story of Moses, the Israelites' escape from Egypt, and God's agreement (covenant) with them. God gives the Law at Mount Sinai and the tabernacle is constructed.

LEVITICUS

This book containes the laws, which God's people should keep to please and worship him.

NUMBERS

The people of Israel wander for years in the desert. God prepares them for the Promised Land.

DEUTERONOMY

Before he dies, Moses underlines to the Israelites the importance of the covenant and the Law.

JOSHUA

This book tells the story of the Israelites' conquest of the land of Canaan. They then divide the land among their tribes.

The prophet Elijah prays for fire from heaven to consume the sacrifice on Mount Carmel.

JUDGES

This is the history of the Israelites. They learn that if they turn away from God, their enemies overpower them. They repeatedly repent, after which a leader ("judge") saves them.

RUTH

This is a story of love in the lives of ordinary people, who become ancestors of David and of Jesus.

1 SAMUEL

The history of Israel is recorded from the rule of Samuel, the last judge, to the reign of Saul, the first king.

2 SAMUEL

This covers the story of King David's reign over Israel.

1 & 2 KINGS

These books are about the last days of King David's reign through to King Solomon, the division of the Kingdom of Israel, and the story of the rulers of both kingdoms (Judah and Israel) through to the release of King Jehoiachin from prison in Babylonia, about 561 BC.

1 & 2 CHRONICLES

This is the history of the kingdoms of Judah and Israel. The books give the genealogies and history from the reigns of David and Solomon through to the captivity of the Jewish people in Babylonia.

EZRA

This story recounts the return of the Jews from captivity in Babylon, and the rebuilding of the Temple in Jerusalem.

NEHEMIAH

This book is another version of the return from exile. The walls of Jerusalem are rebuilt and the covenant is renewed.

ESTHER

This story is about a Jewish woman who became Queen of Persia and saved her people from destruction.

Archers are depicted on glazed tiles from the Ishtar Gate of ancient Babylon.

JOB

This story is about the sufferings and the faith of a good man. Job learns to accept the sometimes baffling will of God.

PSALMS

This is a collection of poems, prayers, and praises written by David and others. Many were used in worship in the Temple.

David the shepherd boy plays his lyre.

PROVERBS

These are wise and practical sayings of King Solomon and other learned men.

ECCLESIASTES

This book discusses how the search for happiness and satisfaction in earthly things – apart from God – always ends in emptiness.

SONG OF SOLOMON

This is a song of love.

ISAIAH

These prophecies are about Judah and Jerusalem. The messages are about God's people being saved and hope for a Messiah.

JEREMIAH

The fall of Judah, the people's sufferings, and the final overthrow of their enemies are predicted in these prophecies.

LAMENTATIONS

This expression of grief is about the fall of Jerusalem and the destruction of the Temple.

EZEKIEL

This provides God's judgement on the Jews, and messages of comfort in their captivity.

DANIEL

This story tells of some of the events during the captivity in Babylon. There are prophecies about Christ and the Last Times.

HOSEA

The prophet Hosea's grief about his unfaithful wife illustrates God's sadness about Israel.

JOEL

This prophesies God's judgement of Judah and the blessings that will follow a U-turn (repentance).

AMOS

This warns of God's judgement of Israel because of idol worship and bad treatment of the poor. God also judges surrounding nations. There are glimpses of the Messiah's kingdom.

OBADIAH

This writing predicts that Edom will be destroyed, and promises that Zion (Israel) will be saved.

JONAH

This is the story of the prophet Jonah, showing God's concern for nations that repent.

MICAH

This warns of judgement on Israel and Judah, but also predicts their restoration, and the reign of the Messiah.

NAHUM

This writing predicts the downfall of Assyria.

HABAKKUK

This prophet predicts Babylon's invasion, but foretells Babylon will later be destroyed and God's people restored.

ZEPHANIAH

This prophet predicts the overthrow of Judah because of idol worship, pride, and greed. He foretells God's people will finally be restored.

HAGGAI

This writing predicts the Temple will be rebuilt.

ZECHARIAH

The rebuilding of the Temple, the coming of the Messiah, and the triumph of the kingdom of God is predicted.

MALACHI

This book states how God judges Israel's sins, but also predicts blessings for those who repent and the coming of Christ.

A Jewish warrrior defends the city of Jerusalem.

WHAT'S IN THE BOOKS OF THE NEW TESTAMENT?

John the Baptist preaches on the banks of the River Jordan.

MATTHEW

This story of the life of Christ underlines the importance of Jesus' teachings.

MARK

This story of the life of Christ stresses his last week in Jerusalem, death on the cross, and resurrection.

LUKE

This story of the life of Christ emphasizes Jesus the man – and the people whose lives he changed.

JOHN

This account of the life of Christ reveals Jesus to be the Son of God.

ACTS

This story begins with the coming of the Holy Spirit, and tells of the spread of Christianity to many different people and places.

ROMANS

The apostle Paul explains that people are saved by God's grace alone through faith in Christ.

1 CORINTHIANS

In Paul's letter to the church at Corinth, Greece, he corrects their mistakes, points out their sins, and encourages them to follow Christ's love.

2 CORINTHIANS

In Paul's letter of love to the church at Corinth, he encourages them to live in love and unity.

GALATIANS

Paul stresses Christian freedom. People are saved by God's grace alone, through faith in Christ.

Peter mends a fishing net on the shore of the Sea of Galilee.

Jesus of Nazareth teaches his disciples about the kingdom of God.

EPHESIANS

Paul teaches about Christ and the church, which he calls "God's household".

PHILIPPIANS

Paul describes the joy and beauty of the Christian life.

COLOSSIANS

Paul corrects mistakes and wrong teachings. He emphasizes that Jesus Christ alone can save all people.

1 THESSALONIANS

Paul calls Christians to faith, pure lives, and holiness, as they wait for Christ to return.

2 THESSALONIANS

Paul writes about the second coming of Christ.

1 & 2 TIMOTHY

These letters from Paul are about the church and the duties of church leaders.

TITUS

Paul writes to his friend Titus, highlighting good Christian teaching.

PHILEMON

This is Paul's most personal letter. He begs his friend Philemon to accept a runaway slave as his Christian brother.

HEBREWS

The unknown writer defends the Christian faith.

JAMES

This letter is about practising the Christian faith, seen to be alive by the results – "fruit" – it produces.

Temple of Apollo at Laodicea, Asia Minor. The writer of the book of Revelation wrote one of his letters to believers here.

1 PETER

Peter encourages Christians to live purely, as God's chosen people.

2 PETER

Peter warns Christians about wrong teachings, and looks toward Christ's return.

1 JOHN

This writing explains the basics of the Christian faith, which are revealed in Jesus Christ.

2 JOHN

The writing is about the importance of love among Christians and warns against false teachers.

A messenger carries one of Paul's letters to believers in Greece.

3 JOHN

This book tells believers that they must look after visiting Christian teachers.

JUDE

Jude condemns Christians who teach false ideas. He encourages believers to be faithful to Christ.

REVELATION

These visions reveal that Christ is Lord, God is king and will finally defeat all evil.

The Story of God's People

The Bible consists of many different books, written at different times by different people. Yet we can trace through its pages the story of God's relationship with humankind, and particularly with his chosen people, the Jews.

In the beginning, God created the universe, the world, living creatures, and human beings. He placed the first couple – Adam and Eve – in the Garden of Eden, where they lived in harmony with him. But they decided to be free of him and go their own way. This resulted in the "fall" into sin and their exit from the garden.

When humans displeased God, Noah and his family were saved from the great flood that followed by building the ark. Later, people tried to be as great as God by building the Tower of Babel. Confusion followed when everyone started to speak in different languages.

A new nation

God called a man named Abraham to leave his home in Mesopotamia and resettle in Canaan, the "Promised Land". He promised to make Abraham the founder of a great new nation.

Abraham's grandson, Jacob (or "Israel"), had twelve sons, who became fathers of the twelve tribes of Israel. Jacob's favourite son, Joseph, was sold as a slave, but later became chief minister of Egypt. Many years later, the Israelites became slaves in Egypt.

God chose Moses to lead the Israelites out of slavery (the "Exodus") through the Sinai Desert to the borders of Canaan, the Promised Land. At Mount Sinai, God gave the Israelites the Ten Commandments.

Under a new leader, Joshua, the Israelites invaded Canaan and gradually took possession of the land. Through leaders known as "judges" – such as Deborah, Gideon, and the mighty Samson – God guided Israel. The prophet Samuel was the last and greatest of these judges.

The Israelites now demanded a king like other nations, and Samuel anointed Saul. After Saul disobeyed God and was killed in battle, the shepherd boy David became Israel's greatest king, and made Jerusalem his capital city. David's successor, Solomon, built a temple for God there.

Young Samuel helps the High Priest Eli in his duties.

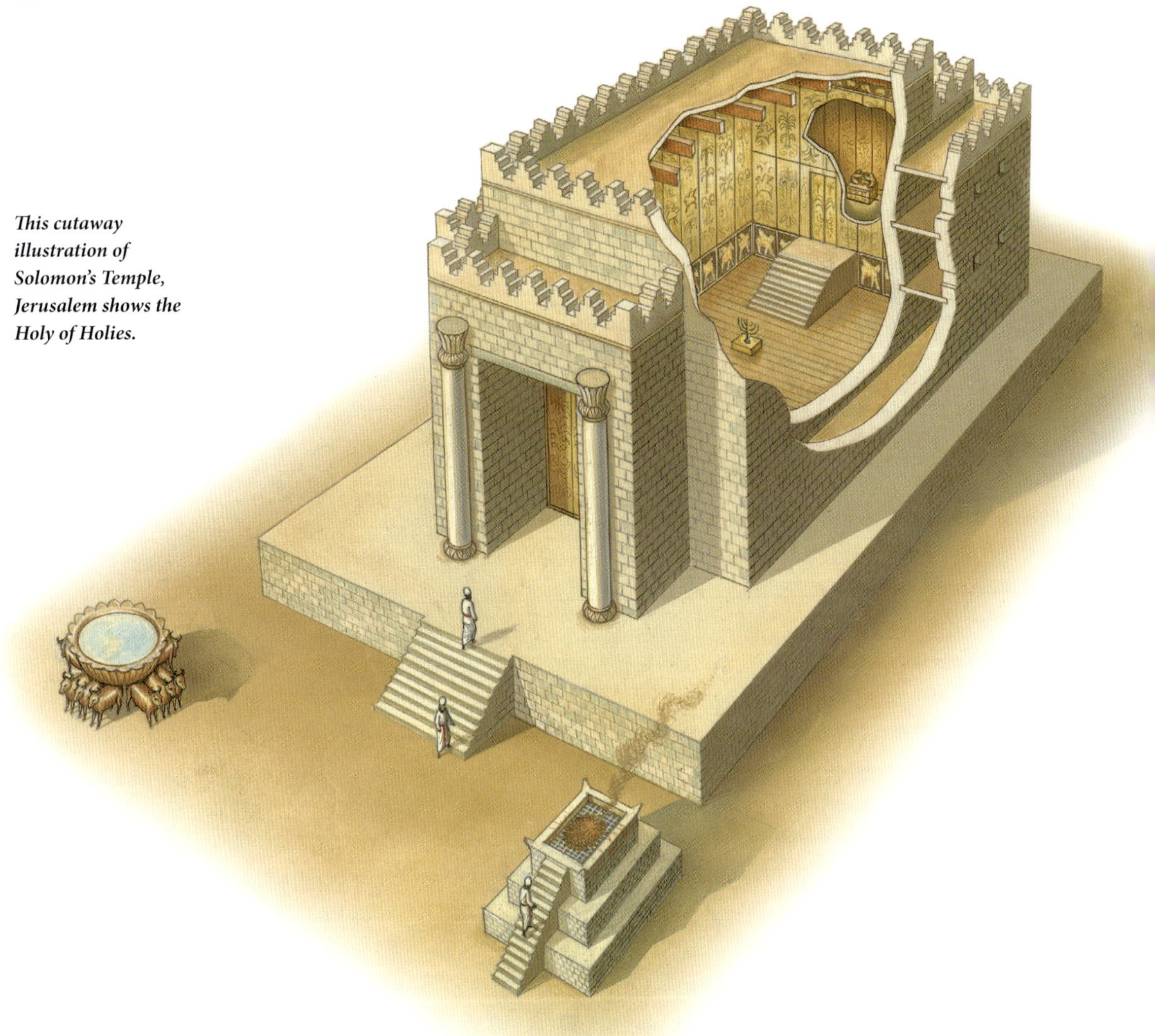

This cutaway illustration of Solomon's Temple, Jerusalem shows the Holy of Holies.

After Solomon's death, the kingdom divided. The south, ruled by his son, was called Judah; the north, Israel. Both kingdoms had both good and bad kings. Increasingly the people worshipped false gods.

God sent prophets to call his people back to him. But the northern capital, Samaria, fell to the cruel Assyrians, and the Kingdom of Israel came to an end.

The prophet Jeremiah called on the people of Judah to return to God. But Nebuchadnezzar II of Babylon captured Jerusalem and took many of its people into exile. The prophet Daniel served at the royal court in Babylon. The prophet Ezekiel encouraged the Jewish exiles.

King Cyrus of Persia took over the Babylonian Empire in 539 BC. He allowed the Jews to return home and rebuild the Temple in Jerusalem. His servant Nehemiah supervised the reconstruction of the walls of Jerusalem.

Alexander the Great of Macedonia conquered the Persian Empire in 333 BC, spreading Greek ("Hellenistic") culture throughout the known world. For 300 years the people of Israel suffered under foreign rule: Greek 331–320 BC; Egyptian 320–198 BC; Syrian 198–63 BC, and finally Roman from 63 BC.

A saviour

God's people longed for the saviour spoken about by the prophets. When Jesus was born to Mary in Bethlehem, God told the shepherds and wise men that he was the promised Saviour-King.

Jesus' cousin, John the Baptist, also announced the coming of the one promised by God.

Young Jesus helps Joseph the carpenter in Nazareth.

Jesus explains to the Jewish leader Nicodemus how he can find eternal life.

Crowds greet Jesus as king as he rides into Jerusalem.

After being baptized by John, Jesus began to preach, teach, and perform miracles of healing and nature. For three years he proclaimed God's kingdom. He chose twelve followers to be his close disciples.

Then Jesus went to Jerusalem. After entering the city in triumph, he was arrested by his enemies. He was tried for claiming to be God, and sentenced to death on a cross. Three days later, his grave was discovered to be empty. He appeared alive to many of his followers. Weeks later, he returned to heaven, promising to send his Holy Spirit to his disciples.

On receiving the Holy Spirit, his disciples (apostles) set out to share the good news about Jesus as Saviour-King. Paul, who once persecuted believers, became a passionate follower of Jesus. He carried the good news throughout the Roman world setting up churches. After several hazardous missions, Paul was imprisoned and taken to Rome. He and others wrote many letters to the young churches.

The apostle John, who wrote the book of Revelation, died around AD 100.

Jesus' family and friends lament his death on the cross.

Where Did the Bible Come From?

Ancient stories were passed on by word of mouth at gatherings such as feasts, weddings, and family meals.

The Bible we have today is usually one very thick book, with more than 1,000 pages. However different parts of the Bible were written by a lot of different people over a very long period of time – probably as much as 1,500–2,000 years. Only later were the many varied parts brought together into a collection of books.

The famous stories about the early Jewish people – Joseph and his special coat, Moses and the Ten Commandments, and David and Goliath – all happened more than 3,000 years ago.

Word of mouth

The first stories in the Bible go back to pre-history, long before writing was invented. These stories were passed on in much the same way as children's playground songs and rhymes are passed on today – by being constantly repeated. Passing stories on in this word-of-mouth way is sometimes called spoken, or oral, tradition.

Around campfires, at worship, at work, or at war, people used to sing songs and tell stories that they had learned as children. Because these particular stories were about God, they were treated respectfully. Every word was important and had to be repeated correctly.

A Jewish rabbi holds up the Torah scroll, containing the books of Moses, in a synagogue.

Making the Old Testament

The books of the Old Testament (The Jewish Scriptures) were first written down over several centuries. The first five books of the Old Testament are called the Torah and were said to have been written by Moses. While some books were written and collected, others were still being passed on through storytelling. The writings were added to, amended, and written to bring hope and guidance to the people.

Excluded books

Seven books, sometimes called the "Deuterocanonical" books (meaning the "second list"), were excluded from the official list of Jewish Scriptures. This left the 39 books that Christians call the Old Testament, although they were originally arranged in a different order.

Today, most Protestant churches use the same list of 39 books, and call them the "Old Testament". However, the Roman Catholic and Eastern Orthodox churches also include the Deuterocanonical books in their Old Testament.

Collecting the Jewish Scriptures

We don't know exactly when all the books of the Jewish Scriptures were finally collected. Some of the writings in the Jewish Scriptures may go back as far as 1100 BC. But the process of bringing the books together probably didn't start until around 400 BC.

The collecting of books continued while new books were being written – until as late as the second century BC. The business of deciding which books would form the official Jewish Scriptures went on until almost AD 100. It was often done by Jewish teachers, or "rabbis".

It is not clear exactly how they decided which books should be considered holy enough to be included in the Jewish Scriptures. We know that around AD 100, a group of Jewish scholars met at Jamnia (or "Javneh") a Jewish settlement west of Jerusalem to debate which books should be included in the Jewish Scriptures.

What about the New Testament?

Jesus of Nazareth was born more than 2,000 years ago. Jesus and his followers were Jewish, so they read and quoted from the Jewish Scriptures.

After Jesus died and was raised to life (around AD 30), stories about his life, death and resurrection, and his sayings, were passed on by word of mouth. About AD 65 these stories and sayings began to be gathered and written down in books known as "Gospels". Matthew, Mark, Luke, and John each wrote a Gospel based on eyewitness accounts of Jesus' life.

Matthew, Mark, and Luke's writings are usually called the "Synoptic Gospels". They all seem to be based on similar spoken traditions about Jesus' life and teaching. John writes in a different way about Jesus' life and work. These four Gospels make up about half of what Christians call the New Testament.

The earliest writings of the New Testament, however, are probably some of the letters that the apostle Paul wrote to groups of Jesus' followers scattered around the Roman Empire. The earliest of these letters is probably Galatians or 1 Thessalonians, which may have been written as early as AD 50.

Which books make up the New Testament?

By about AD 100 all the New Testament books had been written. They were in Greek, at this time an international language in the Roman Empire. These and other writings were often passed around, and read as single books or letters.

Over nearly 300 years, from AD 100 to 400, Christian leaders and church councils pondered which of these writings should be considered holy and treated with the same respect as the Jewish Scriptures. Books were gradually collected together to create an agreed standard rule (or "canon" – Greek for "measuring rod") for the Christian faith. As Christian leaders decided which books should be in the New Testament, they would ask: "Does this teach what Jesus' disciples taught?" and "Does this help Christians in their faith?"

In AD 367 Athanasius, Bishop of Alexandria, listed the 27 books he felt Christians should consider authoritative (reliable). This list was accepted by most Christian churches: the writings he named are the 27 books we call today the New Testament.

Matthew, Mark, and Luke – the Synoptic Gospels – and John.

Who Wrote the Bible?

Moses

David

Isaiah

Amos

Nehemiah

The people who wrote the books of the Bible were a varied bunch. They did various jobs, had contrasting personalities, and wrote in different styles, languages, and forms.

Some Old Testament Writers

Moses

Moses' parents were Israelites in Egypt. As a baby, he was rescued from death by Pharaoh's daughter, and grew up as her son, a prince of Egypt. Later God chose Moses to lead the Israelite slaves to freedom (the Exodus). Moses is said to have written the first five books of the Bible. In the Jewish religion, these are called the Books of the Law, or the Torah.

David

David was the shepherd boy who killed the giant Goliath with a stone from his sling. He grew up to become a great warrior and Israel's most famous king. He was a poet and musician, and wrote many of the psalms (songs) in the Bible.

Isaiah

Isaiah, the friend and adviser of kings, was God's prophet in Jerusalem around 740 BC. Like other Jewish prophets, Isaiah called his people back to faith in God. In the book of Isaiah we find his message of hope: a deliverer ("Messiah") would come to save his people.

Amos

Amos was a farmer. He hated the cheating, greed, and false worship of God, which he saw in the towns of Israel, and spoke out for God. When he was forced to leave, he wrote down his fierce message.

Nehemiah

Nehemiah was an important Jewish official in the palace of the Persian king. Artaxerxes I gave Nehemiah permission to return to his homeland, Judah, to organize the rebuilding of Jerusalem. The book of Nehemiah includes quotes from Nehemiah's journal.

Peter

John

Paul

Luke

Some New Testament Writers

Mark

Mark was sometimes known as "John Mark". When Mark was a young man, Jesus' friends used to meet in an upper room in his mother's house in Jerusalem. Later Mark helped Peter and Paul in their missionary work. Mark worked closely with Peter and often heard about his experiences as one of Jesus' disciples. After Peter was executed in Rome, Mark wrote down Peter's teaching to form what we know as Mark's Gospel. This was probably the first gospel to be written down. It is sometimes called the "action" gospel because the Gospel has more about Jesus' actions rather than his teachings.

John

John was a fisherman on the Sea of Galilee and became one of Jesus' closest friends. He was an early leader of the church. In addition to John's Gospel, he may have also written the three letters included in the New Testament, and probably the Book of Revelation while he was exiled on the island of Patmos, near modern Turkey.

Paul and friends

After he was converted to faith in Christ, Paul became a tireless missionary. In the New Testament there are 21 letters, mainly written to help young churches and new Christians. Many were written by Paul to Christian groups in various towns and cities. Others were written by Jesus' brother James, by the apostle Peter, and by Jude.

Luke

Luke was a doctor and a friend of Paul. He probably accompanied Paul on some of his journeys. He wrote Luke's Gospel (one of the Synoptic Gospels) and also the Book of Acts, the history of the very first Christians.

How the Bible Was Written Down

Stone tablets

The first permanent writing surface used in Bible lands was stone.

In the Bible, the first time that writing is mentioned is when the Ten Commandments were written on stone.

The first "pen" was a chisel!

Waxed boards

The Assyrians, Greeks, and Romans all used writing boards made from pieces of wood or ivory covered with wax. Sometimes two boards were hinged together.

Any pointed stick could be used as a writing tool.

Hinged boards with wax-covered writing surfaces.

Egyptians make papyrus from reeds grown near the River Nile.

Papyrus

Even before the pyramids were built, the ancient Egyptians had learned to make papyrus "paper" from the inner stalk (pith) of papyrus reeds that grew in marshy areas. (The English word "paper" comes from the name "papyrus".)

The thick, damp stems were laid out in rows on top of each other and beaten until they melded into a flat writing surface. When this sheet had dried in the sun, it could be written on.

Papyrus was expensive to make but it could be reused by washing or scraping.

Egyptians made brush-pens from reeds. They made their ink from plants and other natural pigments, such as malachite and yellow ochre.

Clay tablets

The ancient Babylonians shaped clay into thin, flat, rectangular bricks for writing.

Words were pressed into the soft clay with a wedge-shaped stylus. The clay was then baked in the sun to harden.

Archaeologists have discovered whole "libraries" of these clay writing tablets.

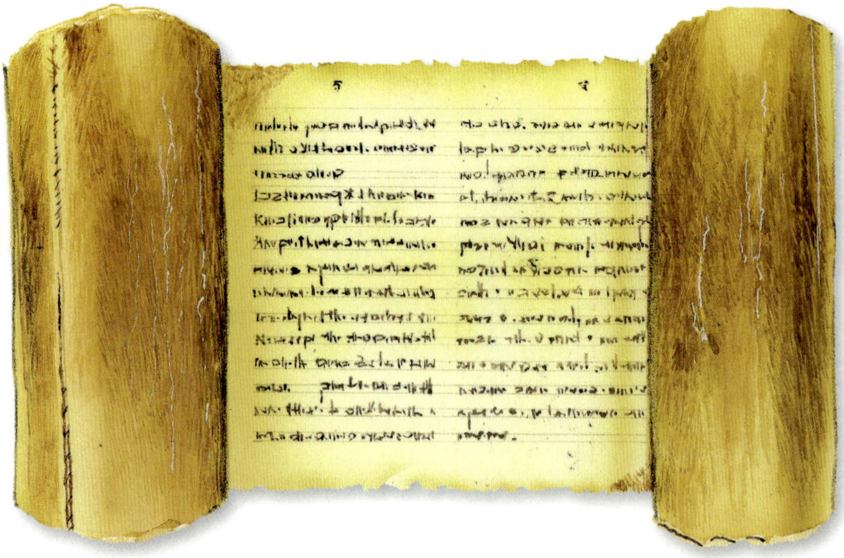

A lengthy scroll manuscript made up from several leather skins sewn together.

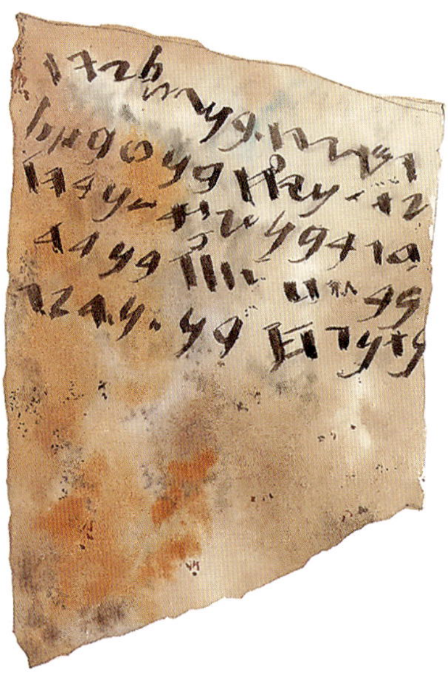

Pottery

People often used bits of broken pottery, called “sherds”, to write notes, bills, and even shopping lists.

They made ink from soot mixed with oil or gum.

Leather

The skins of animals such as sheep, goats, calves, and antelopes were dried, scraped, and cleaned to make a smooth material called “parchment”. (The Hebrew word for book means “scrape”.) The skins were then stretched and beaten flat, ready for writing on.

Pens were made from reeds. One end was cut to a sloping edge and then split.

How to Make Papyrus

Papyrus plants are large reeds, more than 4 metres (13 feet) tall. They grew plentifully near the River Nile, and were also sometimes found along the banks of the River Jordan in ancient Israel.

Papyrus reeds.

1. Cut a supply of papyrus reeds.

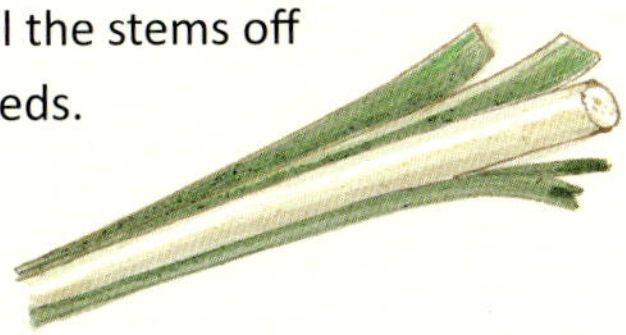

2. Peel the stems off the reeds.

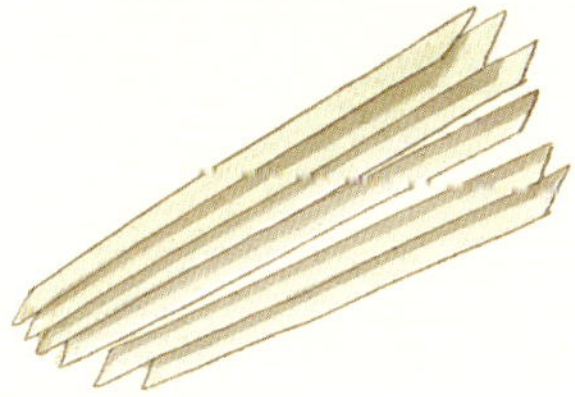

3. Cut the inside pith into strips.

4. Lay the strips side by side, overlapping slightly.

5. Put a second layer across the top, at right angles to the first.

6. Beat with a mallet till the layers form a smooth, flat sheet.

7. Smooth the sheet with a scraper.

8. Join sheets together by overlapping the ends and beating them. The papyrus is ready to use when dry.

How Writing Began

Hieroglyphs – images representing words – chiselled into a wall in ancient Egypt.

Writing

The earliest writing consisted of simple pictures. There was one picture for each word. Writing like this, using more than 800 pictures, has been found in Babylonia (modern Iraq). It is more than 5,000 years old.

Hieroglyphs

The Egyptians made up their own little pictures to represent words, or parts of words. They painted them on papyrus sheets – and carved on walls too!

The first alphabet

In Canaan around 1500 BC the Phoenicians had the clever idea of making up a symbol – a "letter" – for each sound in their language. They discovered they needed around 22 letters – all consonants.

This meant there was no longer any need to learn hundreds of different shapes for all the different words. Any word could be written down just by listening to its sounds and choosing the correct matching letters. This simple idea quickly spread to other languages.

Cuneiform

Unlike the Egyptians, the Babylonians did not have papyrus to write on. Instead they used sticks to draw on damp clay. This wasn't easy, so they simplified their pictures more and more. Eventually, words were represented by standard shapes pressed into the clay with wedge-shaped sticks. The word "cuneiform" means wedge-shaped.

Writing cuneiform on damp clay, using a special wooden stylus.

The Scribe

In earliest times, scribes were the only people able to write and read. Later, when more people learned to read and write, scribes were still needed to do much of the written work.

The scribe was an important person in the town. He acted almost like a lawyer does today. He would sit near the town gate, where business was carried out. He could be hired to draw up a legal document or make a will. If someone needed an important letter written, the scribe would write and send it.

Scribes often also had an important job at court, looking after the public records. They were highly respected. Other scribes had government jobs: making lists, keeping records, preparing accounts, and collecting taxes. Important officials also employed scribes as secretaries.

What Language Was the Bible Written in?

Hand-written page from the Hebrew Bible. Jews often use a pointer, called a "yad" to follow the words, to avoid touching the holy Scriptures with their hands. This yad is pointing to Numbers 6:24–26.

Hebrew

The Old Testament tells the story of the Israelite, or "Hebrew", people. They spoke Hebrew, and most of the Old Testament is written in that language.

The Hebrew alphabet contains 22 consonants, but no vowels. Vowel sounds have to be added by the reader.

Hebrew is read from right to left: the text of the Jewish Scriptures begins at what English language readers consider the end of the book.

The letters of the Hebrew alphabet.

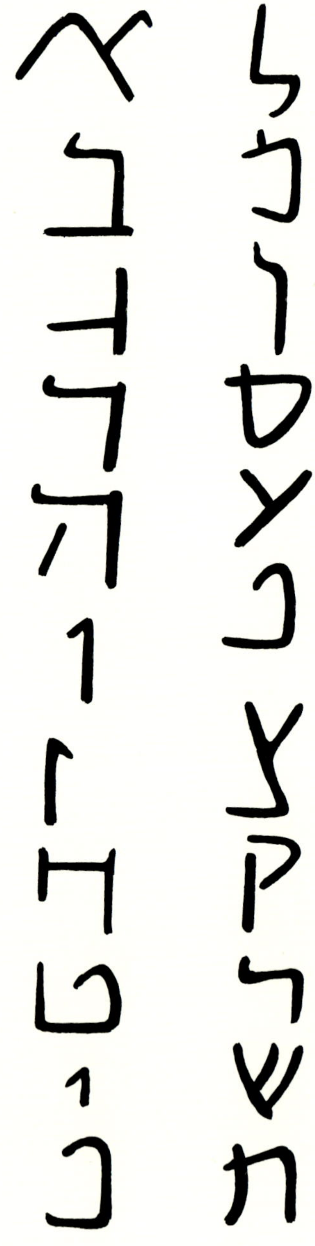

The Septuagint

By the second century BC, Jewish people had spread across the Mediterranean world. They often spoke Greek, rather than Hebrew. In Alexandria, Egypt, the Jewish Scriptures (the Christian Old Testament) were now translated from Hebrew into Greek.

This translation was known as the "Septuagint". There is a legend explaining how the Septuagint got its name. The story goes that 72 scholars began translating the Jewish Scriptures from Hebrew at the same time. They apparently all finished at the same time, in 72 days. And the 72 scholars are supposed to have found their translations were all exactly the same! The number 72 gave the translation its name: the word "Septuagint" comes from the Latin for "seventy".

The Septuagint was the main version of the Jewish Scriptures used by early Christians.

Jesus raises Jairus' daughter.

Aramaic

The Persians were the most powerful nation in the Middle East for 200 years from about 550 BC. They spoke a language called "Aramaic". Traders in this region also commonly spoke Aramaic. Parts of the Old Testament books of Daniel, Ezra, and Jeremiah were originally written in the Aramaic language.

By New Testament times, Aramaic had become the everyday language of Jewish people. However, the Jews still used Hebrew for prayer and worship. Educated people understood Hebrew. But when the Jewish Scriptures was read aloud in services at the Jewish synagogue, a translator often gave the meaning in Aramaic.

Jesus would have spoken Aramaic. When writing the Gospels, Jesus' disciples translated the Aramaic words he spoke into Greek. In just a few places they kept the original Aramaic words. For example "*abba*" is an Aramaic word meaning "dad" (see Mark 14:36). When Jesus brought Jairus' daughter back to life, he said, "*Talitha, koum*". These were his actual Aramaic words – in English, "Little girl, I say to you, get up!" (Mark 5:41).

The letters of the Greek alphabet.

α β γ δ ε ζ η θ
ι κ λ μ ν ξ ο π ρ
ς σ τ υ φ χ ψ ω

Part of an ancient Bible manuscript in Greek. Notice that no space has been left between words.

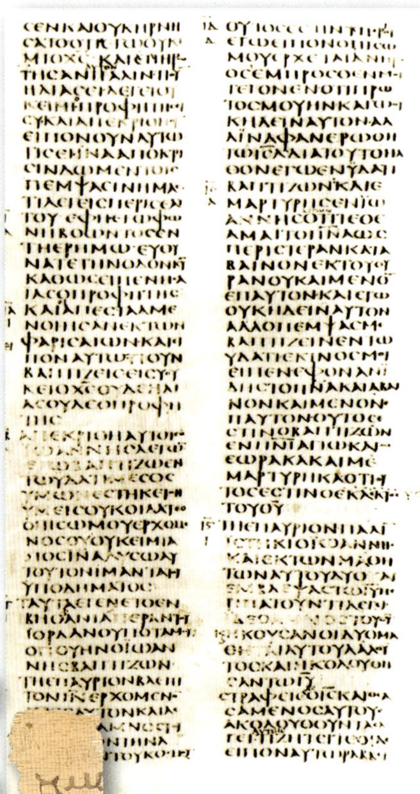

Greek

In 331 BC the famous Greek general Alexander the Great conquered Persia. From this time, he ruled the known ancient world and "common" ("*koine*") Greek became the language that most people understood.

There are 24 letters in the Greek alphabet, which was the first alphabet to include letters for vowels. Sentences and books were written from left to right, as in English.

In the book of Revelation, God says: "I am the Alpha and the Omega" (Revelation 1:8) – the first and last letters of the Greek alphabet.

When the followers of Jesus wrote the New Testament, they wanted all the known world to understand the Good News, so they wrote in Greek.

Below: The earliest known fragment of the New Testament, dating to around AD 130 shows some words from chapter 18 of John's Gospel in Greek.

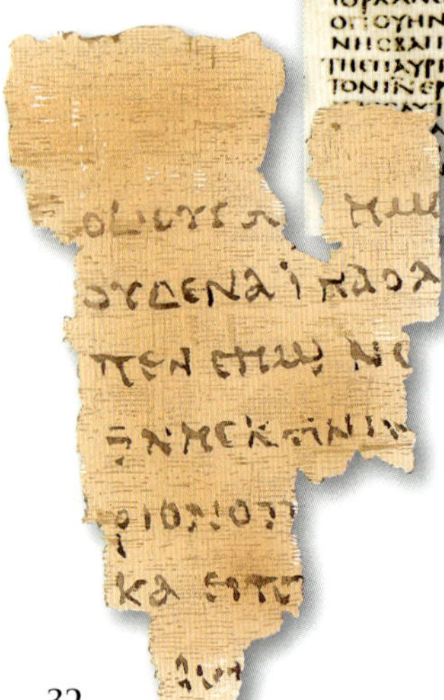

Why Was the Bible Written on Scrolls?

When the Bible was written, books with pages had not been invented. Instead, people wrote on scrolls. These were made from sheets of papyrus, parchment, or even thin sheets of copper, sewn or glued together to form a long strip, up to 10 metres (30 feet) long and 30 centimetres (12 inches) wide. Each end of the scroll was wound around a wooden rod with handles. A reader unrolled the scroll with one hand and rolled it up with the other. When not in use, scrolls were wrapped in cloths and stored in tall jars to protect them.

Paul wrote from prison in Rome asking his friend Timothy to bring him his "scrolls, especially the parchments" (2 Timothy 4:13).

Even today Jewish synagogues keep sacred Torah scrolls of their Scriptures in a special cupboard, known as the "ark".

Hebrew scrolls would be unwound and read from right to left.

These writing scrolls made from copper were found at Qumran, near the Dead Sea, Israel.

Scrolls in Jars

The Dead Sea Scrolls were discovered in caves in these hills near Qumran, Israel.

The Dead Sea Scrolls were stored in ceramic jars.

In 1947 a Bedouin shepherd boy minding his flock in the bare hills west of the Dead Sea noticed an opening in nearby cliffs. He threw a stone inside, and heard the sound of crockery breaking. Intrigued, he went to explore. He discovered a number of pottery jars.

Inside the jars, the shepherd boy found rolls of leather parchment covered in ancient Hebrew writing. At first no one was interested. But when some archaeologists saw the scrolls, they became very excited.

Finally around 800 scrolls were found in similar caves near Qumran. They were probably the library of a Jewish religious group known as the "Essenes". The scrolls include parts of every book in the Hebrew Old Testament except Esther, and have become well known as the "Dead Sea Scrolls".

Part of the excavated remains of the ancient settlement at Qumran, near the Dead Sea.

The Essene group lived nearby around the time of Jesus. They built a settlement that has been carefully excavated. This settlement included a watchtower, a dining room, a writing room (possibly where the Dead Sea Scrolls were copied), baths for religious purposes, a pottery, and a cemetery.

Archaeologists using a method called "Carbon 14 dating" have shown that these Dead Sea Scrolls were written between 200 BC and AD 70.

A scroll of Isaiah contains almost the complete book. It is 1,000 years older than the next oldest surviving copy of Isaiah – yet the two versions are almost identical. This shows that the men copying the scripts took their work very seriously.

These manuscripts, dating from between the third century BC and the first century AD, have helped scholars to understand better the words of certain Bible verses, and to decide how best to translate particular verses or words.

A section of Hebrew from one of the Bible scrolls found at Qumran.

The First Books

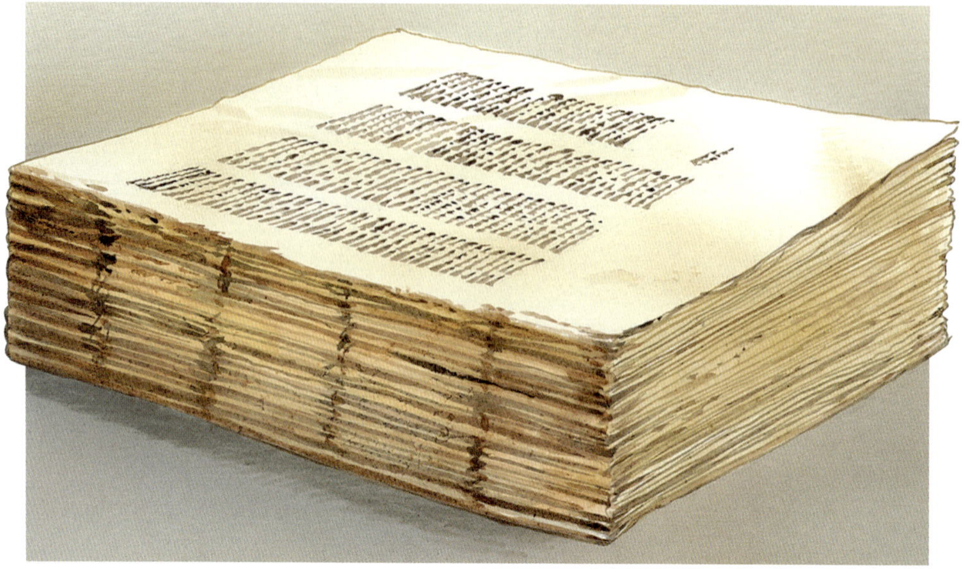

The **Codex Sinaiticus**, *the earliest complete manuscript of the New Testament we have today. It was bound as a book, or "codex".*

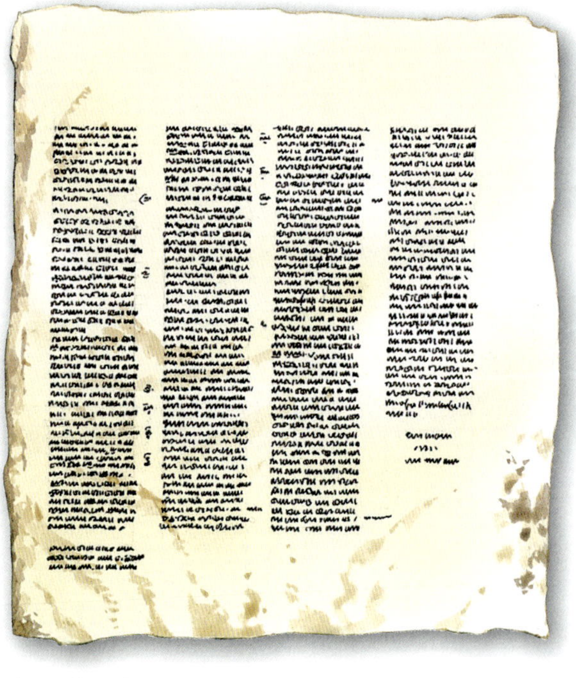

A page from the **Codex Sinaiticus.**

Scrolls were cumbersome to carry. Also, it could take time to find a particular Bible passage on a long scroll.

In the second century AD, Christian leaders collected together the books of the New Testament. Instead of using a scroll, they hit on the idea of collecting together several sheets of papyrus or parchment, folding them in half, sewing along the fold, and adding more folded sheets.

This forerunner of the modern book was sometimes also given a hard cover. This early type of book was called a "*codex*" (plural *codices*).

The book, more or less as we know it, had arrived!

St Catherine's Monastery in the Sinai Peninisula, where Constantin Tischendorf discovered the **Codex Sinaiticus.**

The oldest New Testament

The earliest surviving complete copy of the New Testament was written not long after AD 300.

In 1844 a German scholar called Constantin Tischendorf was exploring the remote and ancient monastery of St Catherine, in the Sinai Desert, Egypt. There he discovered some parchments with early Greek writing. They turned out to be part of the Old Testament, dating to the fourth century AD.

Excited by his discovery, Tischendorf returned to the monastery to see if he could find any more manuscripts. Eventually he found parchment sheets that made up almost the whole Bible.

The manuscript Tischendorf found is known as the *Codex Sinaiticus* because it was found at the foot of Mount Sinai. It is preserved today in the British Library, London.

Other important early manuscripts of the Bible in Greek include the *Codex Alexandrinus*, also in London's British Library, and the *Codex Vaticanus*, now in the Vatican Library, Rome.

These early manuscripts are vital for scholars, who can check that the text that is used to translate modern Bibles is identical to the text known by the early Christians. By comparing different manuscripts, they can see where copyists' mistakes, or well-meaning "improvements", may have altered the original words.

The nineteenth-century Bible scholar Constantin Tischendorf (1815–74).

How the Bible Survived

Jewish scribes carefully copy the words of an Old Testament book. Another scribe is checking a scroll of Scripture.

The very first manuscripts of the books that make up the Old and New Testaments have never been found. They probably wore out from continual use – or were destroyed centuries ago. However, copies of these manuscripts were made and became valued possessions of synagogues, churches, and monasteries. Before these copies deteriorated, new copies were made. Then copies were made from these copies, and so on – from one generation to the next.

Careful scribes

When new copies of Old Testament scrolls were needed, every word had to be written out by hand. Jewish scribes had the sacred job of preserving, copying out, and explaining the teaching of the Old Testament. To ensure that each scribe understood how important his work was, and to prevent mistakes, he had to follow careful rules:

- Each day he had to start his work with prayer.
- He had to leave blank the name of God, to be filled in later by another scribe, using "purer" ink.
- At the end of a section of a book, the scribe counted the lines, the words, and the letters in the original, and checked them against his copy.

Sometimes mistakes were made – but they averaged only one in every 1,580 letters. Often several scribes made copies while another scribe read the text aloud.

Copying monks

Later the books of both the Old and New Testaments were copied by Christian monks.

Men – and sometimes women – lived together in a monastery, spending their days in prayer, Bible study, and useful work, such as farming or nursing.

After the Roman Empire collapsed, monks protected, preserved, and passed on the Bible. When a Bible was wearing out, the monks spent many months making a fresh copy. Every codex had to be copied out by hand. It was a long, painstaking process.

Monks sometimes made mistakes perhaps because they grew tired, or because they were working in poor light. Sometimes the scribe would deliberately change words, because he wanted to put Scripture into his own words or change an emphasis or meaning.

Often the monks worked in a special writing room (or "scriptorium"), each man writing silently at his desk. Because of the danger of fire destroying manuscripts, the writing room had no fire to heat it and no candles to light it.

Christian monks copy manuscripts. Notice the quill pen and the mortar and pestle, with powder to dry the ink.

Translating the Bible

An ancient Bible in the Amharic language, from Aksum, Ethiopia.

When the New Testament books were originally written, the Greek language was understood all over the Mediterranean world. However by the late second century AD, regional languages were becoming popular.

By AD 300 Christian scholars had translated the New Testament into Latin, Sahidic, and Syriac, a language spoken in what is today Turkey.

A copy of the Bible in the Syriac language.

The Syriac Bible was known as the "simple" version ("*Peshitta*"). Syriac missionaries took the Christian message – and their Bible – as far east as China, India, Armenia, and Georgia.

Christians created new Armenian and Georgian alphabets in order to translate and write the Bible in those languages.

Egyptian Christians translated the Bible into Coptic, a form of ancient Egyptian, and the language of Christians in North Africa.

Jerome translates the Bible into Latin

A rather quarrelsome scholar called Jerome, born in northern Italy in about AD 345, became concerned about the mistakes being made by copyists. He travelled widely, learned many languages, and copied many parts of the Scriptures.

Around AD 382, Pope Damasus I asked Jerome to make a completely new Latin

Jerome consults a Jewish rabbi as he works on his Latin translation of the Bible.

The Vulgate, the most popular version of the Latin Bible until modern times.

translation of the Gospels, Psalms, and other Old Testament books, to try to get rid of the many unfortunate mistakes that had crept in.

At this time, most Christians in Western Europe spoke Latin. They found it hard to understand the Greek New Testament. Some Latin translations had been made, but they were poorly written and full of errors.

Jerome went to live in a monastery in Bethlehem and started to translate into Latin the original Hebrew and Greek of the entire Bible. A Jewish rabbi helped him learn Hebrew so that he could translate from the original words of the Old Testament. Jerome's massive task took about twenty-seven years.

Once completed, Jerome's translation eventually became very widely used. It was known as the "Common Version" or "Vulgate". For the next thousand years it was the standard version of the Bible in Western Europe.

PRECIOUS BOOKS

A medieval monk works carefully on an illuminated manuscript.

In the fifth and sixth centuries Irish Christian monks sailed to Scotland and northern England. They wandered from place to place, explaining their faith and setting up new monasteries. These monks brought with them the skills to create beautiful and imaginative Celtic designs. In their remote monasteries, they produced wonderfully decorated Bibles.

Celtic monks bring Christianity and the Scriptures to Scotland.

Decorating the Bible

The Celtic monks made books from very fine calfskin ("vellum") or from the skin of a sheep or goat ("parchment"). After a monk had finished copying out the Latin words in a fine script, another monk carefully checked his work.

In time, instead of simply copying the Latin words, the monks began to decorate the pages too. These decorated books are known as "illuminated" manuscripts.

Sometimes the copyists would add a painted border with an intricate pattern. They would also enlarge the first letter of a paragraph or chapter almost to fill the page, and then decorate it with patterns, flowers, or figures.

Monks used quill pens, made from

The first words of the Magnificat (Luke 1:46) from a page in a medieval illuminated manuscript of the Bible. The artist monk has made full use of gold ink.

sharpened feathers, and simple paint brushes, but achieved amazing results.

The *Book of Kells*

This illuminated book, with the Gospels in Latin, is a masterpiece of Celtic and Anglo-Saxon art. Monks at Iona, western Scotland, began to create it in the seventh century. When their monastery was raided by Vikings, they took the manuscript to Kells, Ireland, for safety. There they completed it. The *Book of Kells* consists of 339 leaves, and every page is richly decorated. One small design, only 1.6 square centimetres (¼ inch square), is made up of 158 tiny interlaced shapes. The *Book of Kells* is today kept in Dublin, Ireland.

The *Lindisfarne Gospels*

In AD 635 Celtic monks set up a monastery on Lindisfarne, a little island off the north-east coast of England. Around AD 700 they copied and decorated what are known as the *Lindisfarne Gospels*, particularly fine examples of illuminated manuscripts.

The *Golden Gospels*

In eighth century France, guided by Alcuin of York, England, monks created a magnificent series of illuminated manuscripts, known as the *Golden Gospels*. As the name suggests, the lettering was mainly in gold, and decoration in both silver and gold, all on purple stained vellum.

Bibles in chains

Most Bibles were far less splendid than the *Book of Kells* or the *Golden Gospels*. Yet it took many years to copy even plain books and bind them in leather. All these Bibles were very valuable, so when they were placed in a monastery chapel or cathedral, they were often chained to the reading desk to prevent anyone from stealing them.

Into Everyday Words

John Wyclif and his followers translated the Bible into everyday English.

In the Middle Ages most Bibles – however beautiful – were still written in Latin. But most people couldn't understand this ancient language. Some Christians became determined to change this, by translating the Bible into everyday language.

A book for the Goths

In the fourth century AD, no one had yet written down the language of the Germanic Ostrogoths. So around AD 350 Bishop Ulfilas translated the Bible into their language and put it into writing.

A famous handwritten copy of this translation is called the Silver Codex (*Codex Argenteus*), which is kept in Uppsala, Sweden.

Anglo-Saxon

Bishop Aldhelm of Sherborne, in south-west England, was the first to translate any part of the Bible into Anglo-Saxon, around AD 700. He made an Anglo-Saxon version of the Psalms.

Abbot Bede (the "Venerable Bede") of Jarrow, north-east England, translated part of John's Gospel into Anglo-Saxon, before he died in 735.

An alphabet for Russia

In the ninth century, Cyril and Methodius, two brothers from Thessalonica, Greece, took the Christian message to the Slavic people living in Eastern Europe. To help in this task, they translated the Bible into the Old Slavonic

Wyclif's followers journeyed around England, preaching from the new translation of the Bible.

language. This language had never been written down. In order to write their translation, the brothers invented an alphabet, which later became known as the "Cyrillic" alphabet (named after Cyril), still used today in Russia and south-east Europe.

Waldo's versions

About 1175, Peter Waldo, a rich merchant living in Lyons, France, took some of Jesus' words literally and gave away all his possessions. His followers, called "Waldensians", translated the Bible into the Provençal language and probably also into Italian, German, Piedmontese (northern Italian) and Catalan, spoken in north-east Spain.

John Wyclif

John Wyclif (1329–84) longed for the Bible to be translated into English so that ordinary people could understand it. After his death, some of his followers translated the entire Bible into English, finishing their work in 1384. This "Wyclif Bible" was officially banned in 1408, but hundreds of copies were made secretly.

John Hus

In fifteenth-century Prague (now capital of the Czech Republic) a man named John Hus (1374–1415) was influenced by Wyclif's teachings. After his death, his followers began to translate the Bible into the Czech language. They published a Czech New Testament in 1475.

John Hus, the Czech reformer. His followers translated parts of the Bible into the Czech language.

The Printing Revolution

Early Bible printers at work. The printed pages were hung up to dry and the type was stored in cabinet.

Around 1440 printing was invented, or re-invented – the Chinese had been printing books since AD 868. By this time the use of local or national (vernacular) languages was more generally accepted for government, education, and religion. As increasing numbers of people began to learn to read, a new demand arose for Bibles in the vernacular.

In Mainz, Germany, Johannes Gutenberg discovered that he could print onto parchment with wooden letters dipped in dye. Using this method, he could make hundreds of printed books, instead of just a single hand-written volume. Gutenberg next experimented with metal type. He had launched the age of printed books.

Right: A page from the Gutenberg Bible.

The first complete book printed by Gutenberg was the Latin Bible in 1456. It was published in two large volumes, with headings and chapter openings printed in red. Gutenberg produced two editions – one on parchment, the other on paper. Although he printed only 150 copies of this first Bible, it still took him two years to complete, since typesetting just a single page took a whole day, and printing ten copies of that page at least an hour.

Other editions followed rapidly, including "poor Bibles" at more affordable prices. The first printed German language Bible was published in 1466, followed by an illustrated Bible by Joducus Pflanzman. Before long, printing presses were springing up all over Europe, from Rome and Paris to Krakow and London. The first printing press in England was set up by William Caxton in London in 1476.

The first printed Hebrew Bible (Jewish Scriptures) was produced by a group of Italian Jews at Soncino, Italy, in 1488.

Statue of Johannes Gutenberg in Mainz, Germany.

Greek Testament

A famous Dutch scholar, Desiderius Erasmus, prepared the first printed edition of the Greek New Testament. It was published in Basel, Switzerland, in 1516. This formed the basis for many modern European translations of the New Testament, including important English and German versions.

Erasmus of Rotterdam (1466 1536), the humanist scholar who prepared the Greek New Testament for press.

A Flood of Translations

Many church leaders opposed Bible translation and encouraged the burning of the banned books.

In the 1500s, the Bible was translated into many European languages. More and more people disliked the behaviour and teaching of priests. Instead they looked to the Bible as the guidebook for their belief.

In 1453 Muslim Turks captured Constantinople, an important church centre. Christian scholars fled to Italy, bringing with them precious ancient Greek manuscripts, never before seen in the West. This helped bring about a revival of learning (called the "Renaissance") and fresh interest in the Greek New Testament and its teaching.

Right: The desk at which Martin Luther translated the German Bible.

German

In 1521 the German reformer Martin Luther was hiding from church leaders at Wartburg Castle. There he began to translate the Hebrew and Greek manuscripts into German. He wanted other people to experience the joy he had found through reading Scripture.

Luther believed a good translation had to be *from* the original language and *into* everyday speech.

He published the complete Luther Bible in 1532, one of the first in the language of ordinary people. Even today

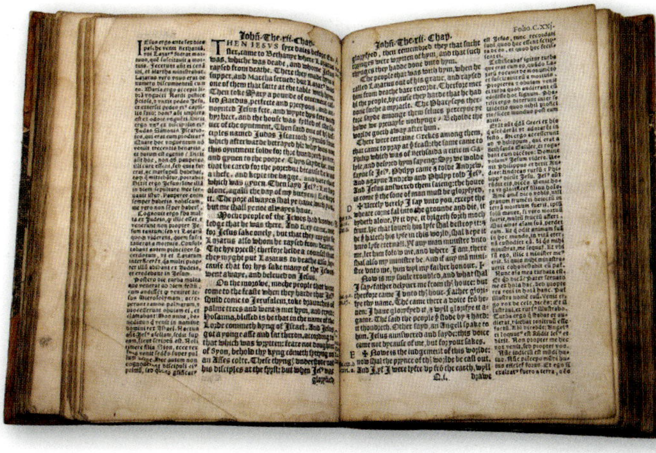

Luther's translation remains the best-loved German Bible.

English

Although Wyclif's Bible had been in English, it was hand-written and contained many mistakes. Even after the invention of printing, English people had no printed Bible that they could read in their own language.

Church leaders thought it was dangerous for ordinary people to read the Bible for themselves and decide what to believe. So it was illegal to translate or print any part of the Bible. The scholar William Tyndale was determined to and he dared say to a priest, "If God spares my life… I will cause the boy that drives the plough to know more of the Bible than you do."

Tyndale went into exile in Germany, where he set about translating the New Testament from the original Greek. In 1526 Christians smuggled printed copies of Tyndale's New Testament into England, hidden in sacks of grain and crates of fish. King Henry VIII ordered them all to be burnt. However, before Tyndale could complete translating the Old Testament, he was burnt at the stake in Belgium.

The Geneva Bible, published in 1560, was translated by English Protestant Christians in exile in Geneva. It was the most accurate English translation then available, and was used immediately by Scottish churches.

Above: Printed copy of Tyndale's Bible.

Far left: William Tyndale (1494–1536).

Left: Smuggling contraband Bibles ashore by moonlight.

Dutch

The Protestant Christian Jaacob van Liesveldt translated the Bible into Dutch, published in 1526. The Roman Catholic Nicolaas van Winghe also made a Dutch version, completed in 1548.

Portuguese

The first Portuguese New Testament, translated by Joao Ferreira d'Almeida, was published in Amsterdam in 1681. The first complete Portuguese Bible appeared 1748–73.

The French Bible translator Jacques Lefèvre d' Étaples worked late into the night.

French

A priest named Jacques Lefèvre d'Étaples published a French New Testament in Paris in 1523. But church leaders suspected he wanted to reform the church, so his complete Bible had to be published abroad in Antwerp, in the Netherlands, where it would not be confiscated. It became known as the "Antwerp Bible".

The first Protestant Bible in French was published in 1535 in Neuchâtel, Switzerland, translated by Pierre Robert Olivetan. An edition published in 1650, often known as the "French Geneva Bible", became the standard French Protestant Bible.

Meanwhile, a French Roman Catholic Bible was produced by the University of Louvain in 1550, called the "Louvain Bible".

Spanish

The Bible was printed in Catalan in 1478, before any Bible had been printed in either Spanish or English. A Spanish translation by a monk called Casiodoro de Reina, an exile in England and Germany, was published in Basel, Switzerland, in 1569. Reina's translation was revised by another monk, Cipriano de Valera, and re-published in 1602. This "Reina-Valera" version became the standard Spanish Protestant Bible.

Statue of the brothers Cyril and Methodius, who first translated the Bible into Slavonic.

Italian

The very first Italian Bible was published in Venice in 1471. Antonio Brucioli's Catholic Bible was published in the 1530s, and the first Protestant Bible in Italian in 1562.

The most well-known Italian Protestant Bible was Giovanni Diodati's version, published in 1607 in Geneva.

Russian

The first printed Bible published in Russia, in 1581, was in Slavonic, based on the translation originally made in AD 863 by the brothers Cyril and Methodius. The New Testament in Russian appeared in 1821 and the Old Testament in 1875.

Swedish

In 1541 Sweden obtained the "Uppsala Bible", translated by Laurentius Petri, Archbishop of Uppsala.

Some of the translators present King James I of England with chapters from the King James Version of the Bible.

THE HOLY BIBLE,
Conteyning the Old Testament,
AND THE NEW

Anno Dom. 1611

Title page of the King James Bible.

Danish

The first Danish version of the New Testament was published in 1524. The standard Danish version, published in Copenhagen in 1550, was named the "King Christian III Bible", after the king of Denmark.

The King James Version

In 1603, when King James I came to the English throne, he encouraged the preparation of a new edition, based on two previous English Bibles (Wyclif and Geneva), and on the Greek and Hebrew original texts.

Fifty scholars worked in six teams to create the King James Version, first published in 1611. This became extremely popular because it was accurate and used language beautifully. For more than 300 years it was the most widely read Bible in the English-speaking Protestant world.

To the New World and Beyond

The English Baptist William Carey translates the Bible into Bengali.

Having translated the Bible into most European languages, Christians in Europe started to look outwards, to other parts of the world. From the sixteenth century onwards, missionaries began to take the Christian message to other continents.

A Bible for Native Americans

In 1631 an English pastor named John Eliot (1604–90) arrived in New England. Having learned the language of the Native Americans of Massachusetts, Eliot began to preach to them. By 1663 he had translated the whole Bible into the Massachusetts language. This Native American version was the first Bible produced in North America.

The first Indian Bible

In the early eighteenth century some missionaries journeyed to the East Indies. A German named Bartholomew Ziegenbalg (1682–1719) translated the New Testament into the Tamil language – the first part of the Bible to appear in any Indian language. He also translated the Old Testament, up to the book of Ruth. Ziegenbalg's Old Testament translation was later completed by another German missionary, Christian Friedrich Schwartz (1726–60).

Shoemaker and translator

After he left school, the young Englishman William Carey (1761–1834) was apprenticed to a shoemaker. But he also began to study the New Testament and became a Baptist preacher. Carey taught himself Latin, Greek, Hebrew, French, and Dutch. He came to believe that Jesus' words, "Go into all the world to preach the gospel..." were addressed not just to the first disciples – as many people thought in that time – but to Christians in all ages.

In 1793 William Carey set out for India, aiming to take the Christian faith to another continent. He earned his living in an indigo dye factory, but in his spare time learned several Indian languages. Soon he started to translate the Bible into Bengali.

The German Bartholomew Ziegenbalg learns the Tamil alphabet in preparation for translating the Bible into the Tamil language.

Eventually Carey directed the translation of the entire Bible into six local languages, and parts of the Bible into twenty-nine others, including Sanskrit, Bengali, Marathi, and Sinhalese.

Chinese

Joshua Marshman, one of Carey's colleagues, started to translate the Bible into Chinese, as did another Englishman, Robert Morrison. The complete Bible in Chinese was first published in 1823.

Explorers were now journeying throughout the world. Businessmen setting up companies in far-off countries often employed chaplains to go with the traders. A revival of faith in Christ, and the example of missionaries such as William Carey, fired Christians with enthusiasm for mission and for Bible translation.

South America

The first printed Scripture in a South American language was Luke's Gospel, in Aymara, in 1829. This translation was made by a Peruvian named Dr Vincente Pazos-Kanki, who was living in London. An agent of the Bible Society met Dr Pazos-Kanki on a bus and persuaded him to do the work!

Africa

In the early nineteenth century, a Scotsman named Robert Moffat went to South Africa and translated the Bible into Setswana.

A Yoruba translation was supervised by Adjai Crowther, a freed Nigerian slave who became the first African bishop. This version was completed in 1884.

Bibles for the World

Young Mary Jones holds her precious copy of the Bible in Welsh.

Right: The first office of the British and Foreign Bible Society, London

In 1796, in a village in the Welsh hills, a ten-year-old girl named Mary Jones decided to save up to buy herself a Welsh Bible. Her family was poor and it took her six long years. At last she set out to walk barefoot to Bala, 40 kilometres (25 miles) away, where she heard Rev. Thomas Charles had some Welsh Bibles to sell. Exhausted, she knocked on his door – only to discover his three Bibles had already been sold.

Mr Charles felt so sorry for Mary that he gave her his own Welsh Bible. Shortly afterwards, he told this story at a meeting of the Religious Tract Society in London. As a result, its members decided to provide Welsh Bibles at reduced prices. But Rev. Thomas Hughes declared, "If for Wales, why not for the kingdom; and if for the kingdom, why not for the world?"

The Bible Society

Partly as a result of Thomas Hughes' challenge, in 1804 the British and Foreign Bible Society was formed. At first the society distributed only existing translations of the Bible. But soon it began to sponsor new translations.

German, Russian, and English Bibles

By 1904 the Society had distributed nearly 181 million copies of the Scriptures worldwide. Its aim was to "glorify God by increasing the number of people who own, use, value and share the Bible in a language they can understand and at a price they can afford".

Hundreds of translations

By 1800, the Bible had been translated into fewer than seventy languages. By 1900, more than 500 languages had at least one book of the Bible.

In 1946 the United Bible Societies was formed to co-ordinate the work of the national Bible societies, and to help and advise on Bible translation.

God speaks many languages

"If your God is so smart, why doesn't he learn my language?" William Cameron Townsend was selling Spanish Bibles to Cakchiquel Indians in Guatemala when he was asked this question. He immediately started to learn Cakchiquel, so that he could translate the New Testament and show the Indian that God *did* care. It took him fifteen years.

In 1934 Townsend started a training school to teach young missionaries how to live with a tribe, learn and write down their language, translate the Scriptures, and teach the people to read them. In time this became the Wyclif Bible Translators, today the largest missionary society in the world, with more than 5,000 missionaries.

Translating today

Bible translators continue working today, helped by some recent discoveries. For example, many ancient Greek manuscripts of the New Testament have been found during the last two centuries. They offer translators new clues to alternative words or meanings in the Bible.

The Bible is a very old book that has come to us because many men and women have worked hard, copying and studying manuscripts, and translating ancient texts into modern languages. Their commitment has helped keep the story of God's people alive.

Before computer technology, it took about thirty years to translate, check, and print a new version of the Bible. Today the same work can be completed in ten years or less, and at a much lower cost.

The Bible Changes Lives

The life of Francis of Assisi was transformed after he heard some words from Matthew's Gospel.

A simple life

In February 1208 Francis of Assisi (1181–1226) went to visit the town of Portiuncula in Italy. While in church, he heard some words from Matthew 10:7, "Go and preach, 'The Kingdom of heaven is near.' Heal the sick… You have received without paying, so give without being paid." These words changed Francis' life. He gave away his possessions, and – wearing only a dark tunic tied with a cord – set off as a journeying preacher to help people. From this beginning arose the wandering preachers known as Franciscan friars, who were as poor as the people they cared for. Francis drew up for them a set of simple rules, taken from the Gospels.

David Livingstone

The explorer missionary David Livingstone said that he felt supported throughout his travels by words of Jesus in the Gospel of Matthew.

David Livingstone (1813–73) explored the interior of Africa, through jungles and along rivers where no white man had ever been before. He faced terrifying dangers, spurred on by his longing to bring Jesus to Africans and free them from the "open sore" of the slave trade. In 1886, speaking to students, he said, "Would you like me to tell you what supported me through all the years of exile?… It was this: 'I am with you always, even to the end of the world.' On these words [of Jesus] I staked everything, and they never failed."

The "Flying Scotsman"

The Oscar-winning movie *Chariots of Fire* featured the story of Eric Liddell (1902–45), who won a gold medal in the 1924 Paris Olympics. As a committed Christian, Eric Liddell refused to race on Sunday, so was forced to withdraw from his best event, the 100 metres. Instead, he ran in the 400 metres, where little was expected of him, as two other runners had world-record times. As Liddell went to the starting blocks, someone slipped into his hand a slip of paper with the words, "Those who honour me I will honour" (1 Samuel 2:30). Liddell not only won the race, but broke the world record, with a time of 47.6 seconds. He believed his decision not to run on Sunday honoured God.

The runner Eric Liddell was encouraged in his Olympic race by words from the first book of Samuel.

Friend of the friendless

One of most celebrated Christians of the twentieth century was Mother Teresa of Calcutta, who looked after outcast people in India. Mother Teresa was awarded a Nobel Prize for her project, but said: "Faith is a gift of God. Without it there would be no life... Faith in Christ who has said 'I was hungry, I was naked, I was sick, and I was homeless and you cared for me.'" Her life was based on the words of Matthew 25:31–46.

Fresco of Mother Teresa from Tucson, USA

Which Version?

Changing language

For 300 years English-speaking Protestants read the Authorized (King James) Version of the Bible. Recently many new translations have appeared. Why do we need new translations? One reason is that language changes over the years.

Bible versions

We come across many different versions and translations of the Bible. It can be confusing trying to decide which best suits our needs. Some versions sound more traditional, some are easier to understand, while others are designed mainly for worship.

Most versions of the Bible are translated word for word, but some are translated thought for thought, in an attempt to help the modern reader more easily grasp the original meaning.

Here is a brief guide to some of the English Bible versions frequently in use today.

Word-for-word translations

King James Version (KJV, 1611)
Often also referred to as the Authorized Version, this translation was commissioned by King James I. It is a much-loved version in the language of Shakespeare's England.

Douay-Rheims Catholic Bible (DR or RHE, 1610)
This is a literal translation of the Latin Vulgate Bible. Most Catholic Bible versions are based on this translation, which includes the Deuterocanonical books (or Apocrypha).

Revised Version (RV, 1894)
This is a British revision of the KJV.

American Standard Version (ASV 1885, 1901)
This is an American revision of the KJV.

Revised Standard Version (RSV, 1952)
This revision, incorporating the KJV, RV, and ASV is intended for both private reading and public worship.

Amplified Bible (AMP, 1965)
This version of the ASV gives several alternative words for different possible meanings.

New English Bible (NEB, 1970)
This is a more literary translation by the British churches and Bible societies.

New American Bible (NAB, 1970)
This official US Catholic version of the Bible is in modern English.

New American Standard Bible (NASB, 1971)
This update of the ASV is formal in style, but more readable than the KJV. Some think it's the most literal English translation.

Good News Bible (GNB, 1976)
Published by the American Bible Society and originally called Today's English Version, its

simple, everyday language makes it popular for children and for people learning English.

New International Version (NIV, 1978, updated 2011)
This completely new translation from the Greek and Hebrew, uses clear, direct, modern English, making it easy to read and understand.

New King James Version (NKJV, 1982)
This modern language update of the KJV retains much of its traditional interpretation and sentence structure.

New Jerusalem Bible (NJB, 1985)
This is a Roman Catholic, literary version.

New Revised Standard Version Bible (NRSV, 1989)
In this update of the RSV, the language is modern, but the style more traditional than the NIV.

Revised English Bible (REB, 1989)
This update of the NEB is designed for worship and for people from a wide range of ages and backgrounds.

God's Word Translation (GW, 1995)
This version accurately translates the meaning of the original texts into clear, everyday language.

Contemporary English Version (CEV, 1995)
This fresh, simple translation by the American Bible Society is intended to be understood by all English speakers, including those with no knowledge of the Bible.

English Standard Version (ESV, 2001)
This new translation based on the RSV combines word-for-word accuracy with clarity and readability.

Holman Christian Standard Bible (HCSB, 2004)
This is a readable, accurate translation in modern English.

Today's New International Version (TNIV, 2005)
This is a revision of the NIV.

New English Translation (NET, 2005)
This is a new, free, online version.

Common English Bible (CEB, 2011)
This version aims to be comfortably read by most readers, using more familiar words for traditional Bible terms.

Modern English Version (MEV, 2014)
This revised and updated version of KJV is for personal and church use.

Paraphrased versions

These are usually translated thought for thought instead of more literally. They are written in a modern easy-to-understand style suitable for readers of all ages.

The Living Bible (TLB, 1971)
This is a popular paraphrased version for family reading by Kenneth N. Taylor, who began it to help his own children understand the letters of Paul.

New Living Translation (NLT, 1996)
This thought-for-thought translation is similar to TLB, but in more traditional language.
A clear, readable translation that is faithful to the original.

The Message (2000)
This paraphrase from the original languages is written by Eugene H. Peterson, who presents the Bible in a fresh and understandable style.

In Other Words...

Psalm 23, often known as "The Shepherd's Psalm", is much loved in all countries. Here are the opening verses in a number of different languages:

English: King James Version

The Lord is my shepherd;
I shall not want.
He maketh me to lie down in green pastures: he leadeth me beside the still waters.
He restoreth my soul:
he leadeth me in the paths of righteousness
for his name's sake.

English: Good News Bible

The Lord is my shepherd;
I have everything I need.
He lets me rest in fields of green grass
and leads me to quiet pools of fresh water.
He gives me new strength.
He guides me in the right paths,
as he has promised.

German: Good News Bible

Der Herr ist mein Hirt;
darum leide ich keine Not.
Er bringt mich auf saftige Weiden,
lässt mich ruhen am frischen Wasser
und gibt mir neue Kraft.
Auf sicheren Wegen leitet er mich,
dafür bürgt er mit seinem Namen.

Pidgin English (Papua New Guinea)

Bikpela i wasman bilong mi.
Olsem na mi no inap sot long wanpela samting.
Em i mekim mi slip long gutpela gras.
Na em i bringim mi i go long ol liklik wara na mi dring na mi malolo.
Em i givim mi nupela strong.
Na em i save bringim mi long ol gutpela rot, olsem em i tok bipo long mekim.

Spanish

Jehová es mi pastor; nada me faltará.
En lugares de delicados pastos me hará descansar;
Junto a aguas de reposo me pastoreará.
Confortará mi alma;
Me guiará por sendas de justicia
por amor de su nombre.

Dutch

De Here is mijn herder,
mij ontbreekt niets;
Hij doet mij nederliggen
in grazige weiden;
Hij voert mij aan rustige wateren;
Hij verkwikt mijn ziel.
Hij leidt mij in de rechte sporen
om zijns naams wil.

Chinese

耶和华是我的牧者，我必不致缺乏。
他使我躺卧在青草地上，领我在可安歇的水边。
他使我的灵魂苏醒，为自己的名引导我走义路。

Modern Italian

II Signore è il mio pastore
e nulla mi manca.
Su prati d'erba fresca
mi fa riposare;
mi conduce ad acque tranquille,
mi ridona vigore;
mi guida sul giusto sentiero:
il Signore è fedele!

French: Good News Bible

Le Seigneur est mon berger,
je ne manquerai de rien.
Il me met au repos dans des prés d'herbe fraîche,
il me conduit au calme près de l'eau.
Il ranime mes forces,
il me guide sur la bonne voie,
parce qu'il est le berger d'Israël.

Portuguese

O Senhor é meu pastor; nada me faltará.
Ele me faz deitar em verdes pastos
Guia-me mansamente a águas tranquilas.
Ele restaura minha alma:
E guia meu caminho em retidão
por amor do Seu nome.

Japanese

主はわたしの牧者であって、わたしには乏しいことがない。
主はわたしを緑の牧場に伏させ、いこいのみぎわに伴われる。
主はわたしの魂をいきかえらせ、み名のためにわたしを正しい道に導かれる。

Bible Facts

Translation facts

More than 6,500 languages are spoken in the world.

Of these, 2,167 languages have either a complete Bible (355), or the whole New Testament (850) or just parts of the Bible (962).

About 4,333 languages are still without any part of the Bible.

The smallest Bible ever published was the Mite Bible published by Oxford University Press in 1896. Its pages were 28 x 41 millimetres (1⅛ x 1⅝ inches), it was 900 pages long and 13 mm (½ inch) thick.

Bible facts and figures

	Old Testament	New Testament
Number of chapters	929	260
Number of verses	23,214	7,959
Number of words	592,493	181,253
Longest book	Psalms	Luke
Shortest book	Obadiah	3 John
Longest chapter	Psalm 119	Matthew 26
Shortest chapter	Psalm 117	Revelation 15
Longest verse	Esther 8:9	Revelation 20:4
Shortest verse	1 Chronicles	John 11:35 ("Jesus wept.")
Middle book	Proverbs	2 Thessalonians
Middle chapter	Job 29	Romans 13–14
Middle verse	2 Chronicles 20:13	Acts 7:7

NB These figures are based on English Bibles and may vary according to the translation.

Most mentioned Bible character: David (1,118 times)
Longest Bible name: Mahershalalhashbaz (Isaiah 8:3)

Some well-known Bible passages

Creation story	*Genesis 1:1–2:7*
The fall	*Genesis 3:1–24*
The flood	*Genesis 6:1–9:17*
Call of Abraham	*Genesis 12:1–9*
The Ten Commandments	*Exodus 20:1–17*
The Shepherd's Psalm	*Psalm 23*
The birth of Jesus	*Matthew 1:18–2:23; Luke 1:26–2:40*
The golden rule	*Luke 6:31*
Sermon on the Mount	*Matthew 5–7*
The Beatitudes	*Matthew 5:3–11*
Lord's Prayer	*Luke 11:2–4*
Prodigal son	*Luke 15:11–32*
Good Samaritan	*Luke 10:29–37*
The Last Supper	*Matthew 26:17–30; Mark 14:12–26*
Death of Christ	*Luke 23:26–56; John 19:16–42*
Resurrection of Christ	*Matthew 28; Luke 24; John 20*
Ascension of Christ	*Acts 1:1–11*
Coming of the Holy Spirit	*Acts 2:1–21*
Conversion of Paul	*Acts 9:1–31*
The love chapter	*1 Corinthians 13*
The faith chapter	*Hebrews 11*

Mary Magdalene meets the risen Christ.

Rules for translators

When translating the Bible into another language:

- Don't add anything
- Don't miss anything out
- Don't alter the meaning
- Find words that communicate to new readers the purpose and feeling of the original.

Translation teasers

Q. How do you translate "Your sins will be as white as snow" to the people of Tonga who have never seen snow?

A. *"Your sins will be as white as a flock of egrets".*

Q. How do you translate "eternal life" for the people of Konkomba, who do not have a word for "eternal"?

A. *Their word for "to be alive" is "to have a nose", so "eternal life" is translated "a nose that has no end".*

Index